Jav

*Fundamental Guide for Novices
(2022 Crash Course for Beginners)*

Malcolm Eland

Table of Contents

Introduction 1

1st Chapter 2

    JavaScript's Evolution 2

2nd Chapter 12

    JavaScript in Action 12

3rd Chapter 15

    How to Write JavaScript 15

Chapter 4 53

    The Future of JavaScript 53

    Conclusion 55

Introduction

Congratulations and thank you for purchasing JavaScript: Basic Fundamental Guide for Beginners.

The chapters that follow will go over how to program in JavaScript. We'll start at the beginning and explain program logic as we work our way through this broad topic, attempting to uncover as much as possible.

JavaScript is enormously popular. As a result, you're doing the right thing by attempting to learn it. My goal is to provide you with all of the tools and information you need to become an excellent JavaScript programmer in no time.

There are numerous books available on this subject. Thank you once more for selecting this one! Every effort has been made to ensure that this book contains a wealth of useful information. Please have fun!

1st Chapter

JavaScript's Evolution

This book will answer a few tough questions while also assuming you have little to no practical programming experience. The reason for this is that JavaScript is the first language for many people. Many people begin with web development or a recommendation from a friend and discover that JavaScript is one of the "easiest" languages to learn.

Of course, this is a bit of a misnomer; I've taught a lot of people how to code. Some people benefit more from a more abstract and simple language, such as JavaScript. Others benefit more from languages where everything is a concept and is right in front of them to play with, such as Java or C++, because the verbosity helps them understand what they're working on in a better way.

Regardless, since you're here, I'm going to assume you're in the first camp, and I'll explain things with enough rigor that you'll still understand the language well if you're already in the second camp. JavaScript is a simple first language. Actually, it's quite the opposite. It's simple to grasp, abstract, and master. However, there is a certain level of difficulty involved, such as getting out of your comfort zone and learning all of the minor concepts related to programming itself.

So, consider this for a moment. What exactly is JavaScript? A programming language is JavaScript. A programming language is essentially something that allows you to communicate with computers and tell them what to do. We know that computers do not understand English. In fact, they have no understanding of programming languages. When you break it down, computers are only really useful for

Understand things in terms of binary codes, which are a series of ones and zeros. This is where the name of the computer derives from.

Every second, the computer performs millions of tiny computations that you cannot see. All of these computations are carried out using the ones and zeroes present at the very lowest level of the computer, which you cannot see. Knowing this, we've discovered over the years that these ones and zeroes can be controlled and manipulated, first by developing languages that work with the computer's processor (assembly) and, second, by developing languages that serve as the link between the complex zeroes and ones and the programmer.

People interested in programming want to learn languages that aren't absurdly difficult to use and understand as computers have become more popular and powerful. As a result, as more people began programming as a hobby, programming languages became much simpler over time. Computer processing power has increased over time, and the standardization of an object-oriented paradigm has resulted in the development of far simpler languages.

To understand JavaScript, we must first learn about its history. Bell Labs, a research lab owned and managed by AT&T, existed in the 1970s. Bell Labs was responsible for many significant technological advances. The Unix system is one of the most important, and you've probably heard of it.

Unix was a watershed moment. It was an open-source and simple operating system that was simple enough to market to businesses, developers, and universities all at the same time without infringing on each other's markets. The development of the C programming language prompted this.

The C programming language has a long history, but it was the first simple and intuitive language that almost anyone could understand. It provides a level of abstraction from the system itself, as well as allowing the programmer to scrutinize the system buildup and thus better understand the computer. This enables the programmer to directly manage things like memory allocation, or the amount of memory used by the program to perform specific processes. In short, C enables programmers to gain a better understanding of the system. They are, however, expected to handle a large amount of difficult information and are prone to manipulating the computer's processing capabilities, for example.

UNIX would eventually be rewritten in C rather than the standard Assembly language. This is one of the reasons C became so well-known. This was a huge deal because it meant that any processor capable of running a C compiler, that is, the program that converts human-readable programming code to Assembly code that the computer can understand, could also run Unix. This program can now be compiled on any system with a C compiler. As a result, the program became extremely popular all over the world.

Furthermore, because C is open source, universities frequently teach it to their students so that, even if they cannot immediately compile UNIX for their computers, they can at least modify the code to run Unix on them. Furthermore, Unix benefits C and vice versa because, first, C is taught in universities to allow students to gain experience before taking on Unix courses, and second, Unix includes a C compiler, which makes it even easier for people to write and run code on Unix systems.

This may appear to be an insignificant detail, but it is a critical factor in the overall development of JavaScript and a key component in the development of modern programming languages in general. This is due to the fact that these languages can inspire a plethora of other languages. For example, the extremely popular languages Java, Python, and C++ were all inspired by C to some extent.

JavaScript is no different. However, in that context, consider the computing landscape in the late 1980s and early 1990s. The general public was gradually introduced to

Because of the popularity of both C and UNIX, computers Because of their combined popularity and accessibility, a large number of applications are being developed for a large number of computers, with the number increasing approximately exponentially each year.

In many ways, however, the Internet was still in its infancy. Web browsers, for example, were unpopular and far from technologically advanced. Web browsers were, in many ways, simpler and less sophisticated than web pages themselves.

Currently, web pages are mostly made up of basic text markup rendered in HTML. This book will only cover HTML when absolutely necessary. As a result, a working knowledge of it is assumed. After all, JavaScript is one of the three primary web development languages, along with HTML and CSS. As a result, learning HTML and CSS is beneficial.

In any case, early web browsers were referred to as static web pages. Static web pages are the inverse of dynamic web pages, which are designed to only reflect and render text and images. In general, once a static web page is loaded, it cannot be changed without changing and reloading the web file.

Client-side scripting is used to create dynamic web pages or pages that can be changed in real-time without modifying the web file itself. Client-side scripting refers to allowing changes to occur solely on the browser side of a web page. Client-side scripting, in other words, enables sophisticated logic and dynamic changes to run within the context of the user's web browser. Any changes made to their machine or browser do not necessarily indicate the transfer of information to a server.

Essentially, JavaScript and all related languages are concerned with bringing web pages to life. It's about giving web pages the ability to do things rather than just stand still. For a long time, this functionality was only a glimmer in the eyes of those interested in web development. This is not to say that scripting did not exist before. There was early support for technologies that were intended to

Allow more interaction between web pages. These, however, were very basic. Even in their early stages, graphical web browsers were capable of scripting.

As a result, another browser, Mozilla, was created, which inspired the development of Firefox. However, Firefox was far from being a factor at the time. Officially, the browser was released as Netscape, which was widely regarded as one of the most popular browsers in the 1990s, and if you used a computer in the 1990s, you were most likely using Netscape.

The concept of embedded codes in web pages - that is, codes written in other programming languages that can be inserted directly into and run from a web page - began to gain popularity in the mid-1990s. However, there was still insufficient information available about the process of developing practical embedded languages. Java served the purpose, but it was not simple. It actually died out because it requires a large amount of raw computing power to be used. A better solution was required, one that could be directly embedded into and alter the web page. There was nothing like it.

Netscape decided to develop a scripting language that could be easily embedded and interpreted within the browser itself. The syntax of the language was supposed to be similar to that of Java and C++. This was done to distinguish it from other popular scripting languages at the time, including Perl, Python, and Lisp. A C-inspired scripting language, believe it or not, was relatively new at the time.

The language was originally known as LiveScript before being renamed JavaScript. JavaScript became the language's final name from then on, most likely as an attempt by Netscape to capitalize on the success of the Java programming language, which was extremely popular at the time, despite the fact that JavaScript was only syntactically related to Java in some places.

Initially, JavaScript was only used for client-side scripting or the creation of dynamic web pages (as previously discussed). The

A year or so after the initial release of JavaScript, the first server-side implementation appeared. Even though its implementations are far less common than those of the client-side, server-side JavaScript is still used today.

The mid-1990s saw the birth of many now-important web technologies, as well as browser wars. JavaScript, which gained popularity quickly and was implemented by Netscape in their browser, plays an important role in the browser wars. However, Netscape's main competitor at the time, Internet Explorer, did not support JavaScript.

This began to shift in late 1996. It was obvious that a business-wide JavaScript standard was required in order for all browsers to access the World Wide Web. To accomplish this, Netscape submitted their language to a standards board for review and standardization. The language standard, known as ECMAScript, was published in 1997. This standardization became the foundation for many different languages and is now considered a language in its own right. It is a language's standard from which other languages are derived. All of these different derivations are referred to as standard implementations. The most popular is JavaScript, but there have been a few others, such as ActionScript, which was designed for Flash coding.

With the standardization of ECMAScript, JavaScript was finally used by browsers other than Netscape. In the mid-2000s, JavaScript was a lofty goal. During this time, JavaScript and the applications for which it could be used were becoming popular among the general public (particularly developers) following the publication of a white paper that defined Ajax, essentially promising the development of extremely dynamic web pages as opposed to static pages previously. This resulted in the creation of many more technologies that can be used in conjunction with JavaScript, such as jQuery, which remained in use until 2015 or 2016.

Later in the Oughts, there was finally cohesive work done to advance the status of the JavaScript language and force new standards fit for new technologies. Since then, newer implementations and continuous unified updates have been developed in order to create a unified version of ECMAScript. As a result, all ECMA implementations, including JavaScript, resulted in the development of new technical capabilities.

Every year for the last few years, new ECMAScript standards have been released.

Ajax must have been the major breakthrough for JavaScript when developers began to take an interest in and support the language. Today, there is an even greater need for broad browser support, and JavaScript began to compete for that spotlight. It has since become the most popular web scripting language.

JavaScript's history demonstrates that it has overcome obstacles to become what it is today. I hope you enjoyed the journey that it has taken. In the following chapter, we'll go over where we are now and all of the different things JavaScript can be used for.

2nd Chapter

JavaScript in Action

JavaScript is currently used in a variety of different ways in the mainstream web framework. It is implemented using various layers such as React.js and Bootstrap.js.

Raw JavaScript is relatively uncommon nowadays, and is only used to build larger projects and APIs. Many of these are open source, and you will come across raw JavaScript when working with these open source projects, rather than in your raw code.

jQuery was once one of the most popular JavaScript libraries, if not the most popular, for a long time. It can still be found on occasion, but it has largely been surpassed by other, more popular web frameworks.

This chapter introduces the most common application of JavaScript, its implementation alongside other Ajax interfaces, and various web-based frameworks that allow you to create stunning and dynamic web pages. As previously stated, raw JavaScript is not widely used, but it will present you with numerous challenges.

JavaScript is also frequently used in conjunction with HTML5 and CSS3 to create browser-based games. As web pages become more capable of running complex animations, these are becoming more popular. Because it allows the creation of client-side scripts, JavaScript serves as an excellent catalyst for all of these.

Don't get me wrong: understanding how JavaScript works is extremely useful. This knowledge can serve as a springboard for other endeavors. After you finish this book, I recommend that you read investigating the various JavaScript-based web frameworks There are numerous examples.

React.JS, Meteor.JS, Mithril.JS, and Vue.JS are all very popular because they make it simple to create interactive and dynamic web pages. In today's world, this is an extremely useful utility that will greatly benefit you as a programmer.

Node.JS also provides a solid server-side scripting implementation. Despite being much younger than PHP, it can compete as one of the more popular web-based server-side technologies. If you want to run your servers and queries efficiently and build broad web-based applications, Node.JS is the way to go.

Now we'll go over how to program in raw JavaScript, which will get you ready to use any of these. It is critical to have a solid programming foundation.

3rd Chapter

How to Write JavaScript

In this chapter, we'll begin to look at how to program in JavaScript. This chapter covers a lot of ground. So, we'll start with the fundamentals and work our way up as we cover all of the different topics and try to get a sense of what this language is capable of. By the end of this chapter, you will have a solid understanding of a variety of programming concepts. Strap in tight because this is where the majority of the book will come in.

Getting Started

JavaScript installation is extremely simple. JavaScript is available if you have a web browser. That's all there is to it. JavaScript implementation engines are built into web browsers, as are any other programs that claim to run JavaScript, such as the game engines we mentioned.

This means that running JavaScript requires little effort on your part. However, there is one thing we must remember before proceeding. While you can normally save JavaScript files and work on them that way, you can't debug them in a browser like this. To use your JavaScript in your browser and have your scripts run, you must call those scripts in some way. To make things easier, we'll make an HTML document with the script tags. In a new file called first.htm, enter the following code:

html>

<head>

<script>

document.write("Hello world!\n"); </script>

</head>

<body>

</body>

</html>

Go ahead and save this file and then open it in the web browser of your choice. You'll see the following:

Hello world!

With this, bravo! You've written your first JavaScript script. So, you may be wondering, what is the essential difference between putting data within your file's head tags and your file's body tags?

In HTML, the head tag is usually reserved for any programmatic logic. You can also put the script in your body tag and it will work just fine. However, rather than being confined in the same HTML document, the JavaScript is usually saved to a separate file and then loaded into the web page from there. This is the most basic method of simulating this type of functionality within the constraints that we've currently developed.

Variables and Data

At this point, we'll discuss a more substantial concept: the concept of data, value, and variables. You'll see these all the time in programming. As a result, it's critical that we start talking about it. This may or may not be relevant depending on how and why you intend to use JavaScript. It will still come up, for example, if you intend to focus primarily on modern web development, but in a more abstracted form. Nonetheless, it is critical that we cover this concept because it is foundational to almost all programming, as well as being instrumental in understanding some of the later concepts that we will be covering. As a result, we'll just assume that we need to learn it and do it.

So, before we go any further, let's start with a simpler question: what is a value? To understand the other concepts presented here, you must first understand how computers process data. As we stated in the first chapter, computers do not understand things in the same way that humans do. After things have been abstracted into things that resemble nothing like the value we gave, they process things in a series of mathematical equations. For example, the bitwise representation of any given number will not be identical to the number passed in. Similarly, when working with characters and text on-screen, computers have no innate understanding of what any of this is or how it can be used; they lack our innate capacity for language. They only understand calculations. As a result, they require a method for converting these abstract human concepts into smaller numbers with which they can work.

However, this is neither an answer nor a question. It only serves as a starting point. The point I'm trying to make is that, in the end, computers understand various representations of ideas in various ways.

Whether those ideas are numbers, letters, or anything else from which an abstract idea can be formed.

All of these abstract ideas combine to form the nucleus of a larger concept - the concept of value. A value is any abstract representation of a concept. That value could be a number, a character, a string, or none of the above. A value is the expression of an abstract idea that can be expressed.

Computers recognize these values based on the type of value they are. Computers require various types because, once again, all of the values that a computer can understand must be converted from our abstract concept of these values into something that the computer can work with, namely ones and zeroes. These distinct types of data are referred to as data types.

There are numerous data types available in JavaScript, and you can even create your own. However, data types are similar to atoms in that if you break down a molecule composed of different atoms, you eventually get singular atoms and can't go any further without getting to the subatomic level and dealing with things like particles and quarks and so on.

Data types in JavaScript and programming in general are somewhat similar. Every programming language has these nucleic data types, which serve as the foundation for all other types of data in the language. These types that cannot be further subdivided are known as primitive types, and each language has its own primitive types.

JavaScript has six different primitive types, each with its own set of use cases and definitions. Here, we'll go over what these various primitive types are, so you can understand what they can do and what kinds of data you can store and manipulate in JavaScript.

String – String denotes a data type that must be made up of only characters. Character refers to anything alphanumeric or symbolic in this context. Essentially, a character is any text that can be displayed on a computer screen. String explicitly refers to the concept of these characters rather than the characters themselves. For example, if you have a string value that contains numbers, you cannot add a given number to it because the system will interpret the string numeric value as a set of characters that represent numbers rather than numbers themselves. When we get to the topic of arrays, this concept will make a little more sense.

Number – Number is a data type that can contain any number, whether it is whole, decimal, or any other type of number. This distinguishes JavaScript from other programming languages. We'll go over this in greater detail later, but it's a fairly simple concept to grasp, so don't worry too much about it.

Undefined – Undefined is the data type that corresponds to any variable (which we'll discuss in a moment) that does not yet have a value assigned to it. Undefined can also be returned in a given function, but we'll cover that when we talk about functions in general.

Null – In computer science, null refers to any number that does not have a value. Null differs from undefined in that undefined values haven't yet had a value assigned to them, whereas null has no value assigned to it.

Boolean – Booleans are another concept that will make more sense later on, but for now, just think of booleans in terms of true or false. Booleans are thus a slightly more difficult concept to fully grasp, despite their apparent simplicity.

Symbol – Symbols are the most difficult primitive for a beginner to understand, and frankly, you won't need to know about them as a beginner. So you can put them aside for the time being. However, we had to cover it out of necessity.

All of these have object wrappers, which is a concept we'll cover later in the chapter. I know it appears that I'm introducing a lot of ideas without discussing them, but don't worry. I promise we'll get to all of this eventually.

So, what is the significance of this information? What can one do with this information? You can certainly accomplish a great deal. For instance, let us change the code we had so that the document. The following is an example of a write line:

```
document.write(4 + 3);
```

Save your file and refresh the page. You should be seeing the following:

```
7
```

See how intuitive that is? You can manipulate these pieces of data. We'll get to that in just a second after we talk about *variables*. Now that you know how data works, you're somewhat prepared to start working with this next concept. See, sometimes, obviously, you're going to want to keep data for more than just one instance as we did above. In these cases, you need a way to keep track of data.

This functionality is offered to you through *variables*. You can keep track of data using variables and then change the data later by referring to it by some name that you define. You can define variables in JavaScript as the following:

```
var variableName;
```

You can also define it with an initial value. This is called initialization:

var myBananas = 3;

Alternatively, you can declare a variable and then define its value later:

var myBananas;

myBananas = 3;

So, what is the connection between all of this? To begin, we need to discuss data types because JavaScript does not require you to keep track of what type of data a variable contains. This is beneficial in some ways because it makes it a much easier language to learn than it would be otherwise, especially when compared to something like C++, where you must explicitly declare what type of data you're working with. Meanwhile, this can be difficult for a beginner who is unfamiliar with how data works and how computers interpret data. So, let's pretend you're just getting started with JavaScript. I decided that instead of throwing you into the fire and expecting you to figure it out on your own, I should explain how everything works. I may have just saved you some time and troubleshooting in the future!

Variables can be printed in the same way that individual data can. This is because variables are essentially just boxes that can hold values. You can change the values in these boxes, but the box will keep the same number of variables and refer to whatever is placed within it. When you create a variable, you're essentially making a box that can hold values. When you refer to that variable, you're saying, "Hey, whatever's in the box with that name, I'd like to work with it."

Let's try this with the last piece of data. Change your script as follows:

>   var number1 = 4;
>
>   var number2 = 4;
>
>   var number3 = number1 + number2; document.write(number3);

Save it and reload the page; you'll end up with the following:

8

If that's the case, then perfect! You're well on your way to being adept at JavaScript. This is only the beginning, but much more can be done from here.

You can create a string variable by assigning a value with quotes around it; quotes indicate that a value is a string value. Note, too, that when you create these variables in JavaScript, they aren't created as the primitives but rather as the object wrappers – which, again, we'll talk about more in-depth later. When you try to connect strings, you do what's called a *concatenation*, which is where the characters from both of the strings are put together into one bigger string.

Anyhow, it's time that we move on to the next major part of this chapter, which uses all the knowledge we gained so far. We need to start discussing *math*.

Math in JavaScript

Math in JavaScript isn't all that difficult. It mostly employs symbols that you're probably already familiar with. There won't be much for you to learn here, but rather this section is about taking the parts you're already familiar with and using them to build a stronger foundation.

Math operations in JavaScript are written and performed using mathematical operators. These are frequently very similar to their counterparts in other languages, as well as in math in general. The operators in JavaScript are as follows:

a + b

This is the *addition* operator, as you've already seen. This will add two things together. It can also be used to concatenate strings or to connect them. If you add a number to a string, then the number will be added *to* the string; for example "hello " + 5 would equal "hello 5."

a - b

This is the *subtraction* operator. The subtraction operator is used to subtract one value from another, as you might predict.

a * b

This is the *multiplication* operator. This is used to multiply one thing by another.

a / b

This is the *division* operator. This is used to divide one number by another.

a % b

This is the modulo operator. This is used to find the remainder of a certain equation. For example, 5 % 2 would return 1 since 5 / 2 would give a remainder of 1.

a**b

This is the exponentiation operator. The exponentiation operator will raise a "to the power" of b and return that number.

These are the basic mathematical operators of JavaScript. You can use these to easily perform complex mathematical operations in JavaScript. This may not seem like a big deal right now, but as we press on through the chapter, you'll see why math, more or less, is essential in anything you may do with JavaScript (or programming in general).

The assignment operators are also important to understand. You can change a value in shorthand by using the assignment operators.

Assignment operators take a variable and then use any of the above operators with an equals sign to perform the assignment. This will give that variable a new value. The equals sign is the most obvious assignment operator, and it is used to assign a value to the left variable on the right side of the expression.

a += b

This is equal to a = a + b.

a -= b

This is equal to a = a - b.

a *= b

This is equal to a = a * b.

a /= b

This is equal to a = a / b.

a %= b

This is equal to a = a % b.

There are two more shorthand operators, the increment and decrement operators. These can be used to add or subtract one from a given variable, *a++* and *a--*, respectively, where *a* is the name of the variable that you're trying to increment or decrement.

We've covered most of the basic arithmetic and assignment operators that you're going to need for JavaScript. Now we're going to use this knowledge to build a foundation for understanding programmatic logic, which is a great and important foundation for being able to use all these.

Foundations of Logic

So, why should we concentrate on logic in particular? What are we going to gain from it? The simple answer is that understanding logic allows you to teach logic to your computer. All logic can be expressed mathematically, and your computer may come to understand logic in this way as well. After all, computers are excellent at solving equations and making comparisons as a result of those equations.

This may not appear to be a big deal, but computers being able to think is a big deal. Consider this: any time your program can make a technical decision, it is using logic. You might not have to think all that hard. There are numerous basic examples of logic. This will become clearer later.

So, exactly what is logic? Logic is, in some ways, just a systematic way of using statements. These assertions can then be used to draw conclusions. In both computing and real life, logic is frequently used to determine whether a given statement is true or false.

The old Socratic form of logic is perhaps the most classic: "All men are mortal; Socrates is a man; therefore, Socrates is mortal." This type of transitive logic underpins much of what we know about modern logic and is perhaps one of the best examples of simple applications of logic in various contexts.

Expressions are commonly used in computer logic. You might remember expressions from high school or college algebra classes, where you had to write out a statement and determine whether it was true or false. You can use algebra to simplify these expressions simply by treating the expression operator as an equals sign.

This basic structure remains constant. Expressions are essentially a method for comparing one value to another. You can specify the comparison standard, such as whether you want to know if two values are equivalent or not, or if one is greater or less.

than the other, and so forth. Expressions, therefore, are a great tool used in logic and play a part likewise in computer-based logic.

You form expressions through the use of logical operators. These logical operators are the very basis of expressions. The following are the logical operators that you can use in JavaScript:

a == b

This will compare value *a* to value *b* and return whether or not the two are equal to each other. If so, it will return true and false if otherwise.

a === b

This will compare the two values and return true if they are both equal to each other *and* if they are of the same type.

a != b

This will compare the two values and return true if they are *not* equal to each other *or* if they are not of the same type. This is logical *or*. So, they can be both *unequal* and *of the same type,* and it will still return true. I'll explain that later.

a > b

This will determine if a is greater than b.

a < b

This will determine if a is less than b.

a >= b

This will determine if a is greater than or equal to b.

a <= b

This will determine if a is less than or equal to b.

You can use these to form *individual expressions*. You can then use these expressions in logical statements, which will be discussed later. Note how these expressions return either true or false depending on whether they're true or not. This goes back to the boolean values that we discussed earlier. These return a boolean value, which may be either true or false depending on the statement.

Let's return to variables for a second. You can store a boolean value to a variable, like the following:

val myBool = true;

However, you can also store an *expression* to a variable, and it will store the true or false boolean value.

val myBool = 3 > 5;

The preceding would be incorrect because 3 is not greater than 5. Because the function of expressions is to compare values, you can compare any values. You can also compare variables rather than raw values. Check that all of your variables are of the same type. If not, your comparison may yield unexpected results!

In any case, you can combine these expressions into a longer expression to create more complex logical systems. These systems will check every part of the larger expression to see if the logic behind it is correct.

There are three more logical operators that we haven't covered yet that are specifically designed to allow you to construct these larger expressions.

expressionA && expressionB

This is the logical *and* operator which checks if both expressions A and B are true. If so, the entire expression will return true and false if otherwise.

expressionA || expressionB

This is the logical *or* operator which checks if *either* expression A *or* B is true. If neither is true, then the entire expression will return false. If either expression is true, then the entire expression will return true. If technically, one expression is true and the whole expression is true, then both expressions may be true since the technical limitation shows that either side is true and that it is satisfied even if both sides are true.

!(expression)

Not the operator, but the logical. You can use this to see if something is false. If it is not true, the entire expression returns true. If it is true, the expression as a whole will return false.

Please keep in mind that you must use the exact version that I've specified. Getting two equals signs but only using one will significantly change the meaning of your expression. Similarly, using only one ampersand (&) or one pipe (|) sign will change the meaning of your expression at its core by transforming it into a bitwise expression, which means it will evaluate things at the bit level or the smallest mathematical level that your computer allows you access to. You won't get the desired results unless you specifically try to do bitwise operations, which you almost certainly won't be able to do at this point. Just be careful when using these expressions.

With that said, hopefully we've established a solid foundation of logical comprehension. This is significant because it will play a significant role in the subsequent sections of the chapter where we discuss the actual meat of control flow and all of the topics that comprise it.

Conditional Statements in Control Flow 101

That foray into control flow begins right now. We'll go over how to construct conditional statements using the expressions we covered in the previous section of this chapter. The first essential component of control flow is conditional statements.

You're probably wondering what control flow is. Control flow is a method for directing your computer to obtain rudimentary forms of logic. You can direct your computer by using the control flow.

(for example, your web page) to make various decisions based on the current state of the provided data.

Active and passive conditionals are the two types of conditional statements. The most basic form is passive conditionals. As a result, we'll start with those.

Passive conditionals work by evaluating a single expression and then taking action if it is true. If it is true, the code contained within will be executed. If the condition is evaluated and found to be false, the code will be skipped.

A passive conditional in control flow takes the following basic form:

if (expression) {

// code within

}

As previously discussed, expression is any constructed expression. This is known as a passive conditional because it allows you to create a statement that does not require anything from the interpreter on the other end. For example, if the condition is false, your interpreter is not required to run any code. This means that the condition can be skipped entirely if necessary.

However, there will be times when you want something different from your statement. For example, if the code runs and the statement isn't true, you can have a backup code that runs in place of the conditional code. This ensures that an action is always taken regardless of what happens, and it also allows you to create a "backup" clause for your conditional statement by implementing another condition.

The syntax for the active conditional is as follows:

if (expression) {

code goes here

} else {

    code

}

The expression will be evaluated as a result of this. If the expression is not true, the program will proceed to the else statement, run the code within it, and then proceed to the next section of the program, rather than skipping over the conditional statement entirely.

However, you may want to have another condition to evaluate at times. This is very simple to set up. You can accomplish this by using else if statements. Else if statements make it simple to create secondary expressions to evaluate. The first given expression will be evaluated in else if statements. If it is found to be false, the second expression will be evaluated. You can create as many other if statements as you want, but after a certain point, it will stop creating them over and over.

You can set up an *else if* statement as follows:

if (expression) {

    // code goes here

} else if (expression) {

    // code goes here

} else {

        // code goes here

    }

That is how you set up active conditionals in order to ensure that some codes will always run in a conditional statement. However, take note that this is not always what you wanted to happen. There are many cases, for example, where you may just want to evaluate to see if a single condition has taken place and then retain that code if that's not the case. In these cases, it is better to use a passive conditional.

Arrays

Before we jump into the next part of the control flow, let us first discuss another extremely important concept: arrays. Arrays are a foundational part of programming, and they will inevitably find their way into your JavaScript programming. So, it's important that you understand arrays and how they function for you to be able to write better codes over the long term.

What is an array, exactly? An array is a fundamental method of storing connected data together. The use of an array may not be obvious at first. Let's start with an overview of arrays by imagining a world without them. For example, suppose we wanted to save all of the different guitar models we had so we could easily find them later.

We could store the names of the guitars like the following:

val guitar1Name = "Gibson Les Paul"; val guitar2Name = "Fender Stratocaster"; val guitar3Name = "Ibanez s420WK";

As you can see above, this quickly becomes unwieldy. It can be difficult to obtain the information you require. Furthermore, if you are trying to increment through the data for some reason, such as listing all of the guitars you own, you will have to do so sequentially and slowly work through each variable, printing them out one by one.

This is not the best approach. The best method is to use an array. Arrays are implemented in a variety of ways across programming languages, but fortunately, the implementation of arrays in JavaScript is quite simple. As a result, you won't have many problems getting them to work, especially when compared to languages like Java or C++, which have far more rigid definitions and can be more difficult to set up.

Arrays are essentially a collection of data, particularly in JavaScript implementations. Arrays enable you to store all of these in a single location and then refer to them by accessing them from that shared location. In the original array implementation, you can arrange memory in a contiguous manner so that the computer can easily refer to these locations and individual value storage locations. All of the data would be literally side by side, allowing you to work through it piece by piece and access what you need.

Instead of mucking around with various variable names and other potentially confusing factors that could further complicate development

When you create an array, you are essentially creating individual side-by-side boxes of data, similar to the variables we discussed earlier. You can then access these boxes by referring to the box's location. Consider a bank's safe deposit box. You can obtain a specific value by reaching into one of several different boxes, and you know which box to reach into by referring to its index.

How can we do something similar in our own code? What are our options there? As a metaphor, we can create our own safety deposit box and then refer to the box we want to open.

To accomplish this, you must first declare an array (as you would any other value) and then feed it a set of data.

var guitars = ["Gibson Les Paul", "Fender Stratocaster", "Ibanez S420WK"];

See how simple that is? Now you can reach into this code and obtain your data any time you want. Let's test this out by creating this file for ourselves. Erase your current JavaScript and type the following:

var books = ["Moby Dick", "Pride and Prejudice", "Ulysses"];

Let's say we want to print the first book in this set. How are we going to do that? First, we must look into its safety deposit box. A single piece of data from an array is referred to as an element. Arrays are made up of many different elements that combine to form the entire array. These elements are located in various positions in the array, which are known as their indices, or an individual as an index. Array indices begin at 0 for practical computer science reasons that we won't go into right now.

So, if we want to print the first item in this array, we can do so as follows:

var books = ["Moby Dick", "Pride and Prejudice", "Ulysses"];

document.write(books[0]);

If you save this and try to refresh your document, you will see the following:

Moby Dick

Easy, right? Know you can locate all the elements in the array. You can also reassign the value of a certain element by referring to its index and assigning it a new value, or you can use this as a means of printing or manipulating the data at these places. Now, let's say that we want to add an element to the array. How do we do it?

The easiest way is to use the *push* method. You simply call the push method and send it the argument of what data you want to add to your array. Let's test this out ourselves. Write the following code:

books.push("On the Road");

document.write("<br/>" + books[3]);

Save your page and then refresh it. You should see the following:

Moby Dick
On the Road

With that, we've worked through the basics of arrays. You're going to see why this is particularly useful in the next part of this chapter.

Control Flow 102: Loops

What exactly are loops, and how can they be used? Loops are an essential component of logic and control flow. You may not realize it, but you are constantly using loop logic.

Consider this: you're trying to type a text message for your best friend, significant other, or someone else. What are you going to do? It's really easy; just type each character and press send, right? However, this is a loop logic application in and of itself.

Consider this. To begin, you open your messaging app and type a message. Then you begin typing your message. You look for the character on your keyboard, press it, and then double-check that you pressed the correct character. This is something you do for each character. You also check to see if you typed the message's final character. The loop is then broken when you press send and close the messaging app. In terms of loop logic, this is how you can think of many simple activities. We don't think about it much because, let's face it, it's not a particularly enjoyable topic to contemplate. Regardless, it's an essential component of loop logic. As a result, we'll discuss it nonetheless.

There are two types of loops in JavaScript: for loops and while loops. These loops are similar in terms of their basic logic (do something under these conditions), but they have vastly different cases that require us to use either of them. In the following section, we'll spend some time looking at these two loops and their best applications.

Let's start with the most basic: the while loop. The while loop is fairly simple because it simply mirrors many of the topics we've already discussed throughout the chapter, particularly the if statement. The while loop operates by iteratively running the code contained within it. The while loop will evaluate the stated condition and determine whether or not it is still true on each iteration. If this is the case, the loop will be repeated. The loop will continue indefinitely.

until it determines that the loop's condition is not true after all. The loop will end at this point, and the code will proceed to the next point. Hopefully, this is sufficient explanation, but if it isn't, don't worry, we'll be looking at the structure of these now.

So, the structure of a while loop looks like the following:

while (expression) {

// code here

}

Let's say, for example, that we want to count from 1 to 10 using this.

First, we must define our variable just as the following:

var i = 0;

Now, we need to set up our while loop. This is going to run for as long as it is less than 10:

while (i < 10) {

}

On every iteration of this loop, we want to have an *i* increment by one (we'll use a pre-fix so that it prints *i* after it's been incremented rather than a post-fix), and we want to print that increment as well as an HTML line break. The code will end up looking like the following:

>var i = 0;
>
>while (i < 10) {
>
>document.write(++i + "<br / >");
>
>}

The outcome of this code will look like the following:

```
1
2
3
4
5
6
7
8
9
10
```

However, as you can see above, this isn't the best way to go about it. It's a little unwieldy and difficult to understand, and you have to go out of your way to do some things that you shouldn't have to, like defining a variable for the loop before you do it.

Loops are useful for testing singular conditions that will become false in the event of an event. In other words, if you don't know how long a loop will run, loops are preferable. For a loop like this, where you know exactly how many times it will run, an incremental loop like a for loop is preferable. We'll get to that shortly.

As a result, loops are frequently used in the form of a game loop. Of course, game loops aren't just for games. Game loops are so named because they adhere to the fundamental concept of games.

A game loop has a boolean variable that is evaluated with each loop run. For example, suppose you have a boolean called running that is set to true.

In games, there is a win or lose condition that must be met. Until this condition is met, the same thing will occur repeatedly. For example, if a player hasn't been hit three times or fallen in lava, that player is still alive! Because you don't know how long they'll live, you don't know how many times you'll need to run your basic logical loop. As a result, you cannot use an incremental loop. For situations like this, it is preferable to use the while loop.

You can set the variable running to false if you step in lava or your hit counter reaches 3. This will tell the while loop that the game is over and the player has lost. Then you can stop running this internal logic and proceed to the next section of code, which is presumably a game over screen.

This is a vast simplification, but hopefully it explains what a game loop is and why while loops are so well suited to them. While loops are extremely useful for continuously evaluating a function and repeatedly running logic in situations where the actual context surrounding it all varies greatly. If you don't know exactly how much time you'll need to run the code, while loops allow you to check that code for a more dynamic interpretation.

For loops are the inverse of while loops. To iterate through the code, for loops are used. Instead of simply running the same chunk until a given condition is not met, you can define the function's running terms. Don't worry if this doesn't make sense right away.

We discussed arrays earlier, and one of the issues you may encounter is iterating through the guitar variables if necessary. In that context, the explanation of the arrays themselves didn't make much sense either. Let us now delve deeper into that.

Remove your while loop code and then reintroduce the book list code. It should resemble the following:

books = ["Moby Dick", "Pride and Prejudice", "Ulysses"];

document.write(books[0]);

books.push("On the Road");

document.write("<br/>" + books[3]);

Now, let's say that we want to iterate through all these. Remove our write lines so that what remains is our declaration and push method. Then, create a *for* loop. How do for loops work?

For loops work on the basis of iterating through data, as we mentioned earlier. *For* loops have three parts. The first part is the initialization of an iterator variable. This iterator variable serves as the starting point of your loop's "counting". The second part is the condition. This is the condition under which your loop continues to run. This will often be similar to what it would be in a *while* loop of the same function, but sometimes there will be a small change made between them. The third part is the incrementation step. This is the step by which your initialized loop variable moves with every loop of the equation. If, for example, you were to set this to an increment by one (variable++), then on every run of the loop, this variable will change by a degree of one.

The structure of a *for* loop looks like the following:

    for (initializer variable; condition of running; increment) {
    // code within

    }

If we want to print every book on our list, what do we do first? Remember that array indices are accessed through referring to their element. These elements start at zero. By starting our initialization variable at 0 and then referring to the index by the initialization variable, we can move through our whole list of books!

Now, how do we define the running length of our loop? In order to define the running length of this loop, you must obtain the length of the array by accessing the array's *length* property.

Then, you must increment by 1 each time.

With all of that in mind, our loop will probably start to look like the following:

```
for (var i = 0; i < books.length; i++) {
document.write(books[i] + "<br/>");

}
```

Our end code will also look like the following:

```
var books = ["Moby Dick", "Pride and Prejudice", "Ulysses"];

books.push("On the Road");

for (var i=0; i<books.length;i++) {
document.write(books[i] + "br/>");

}
```

Now, save and run this code and see how it comes out. It should look a little bit like the following:

> Moby Dick
> Pride and Prejudice
> Ulysses
> On the Road

With that, perfect! You've made a working for loop in JavaScript. Now, let's talk about functions. Functions are an important catalyst for developing a great working knowledge of JavaScript.

Functions

What exactly *is* a function? A function, to some, may send a person back to memories of their old high school or college math courses where worked with things such as *f(x) = y*. In this function, the function *f()* takes an argument of *x*. The argument *x* can be manipulated by the function *f(x)* to produce the output of *y*.

However, there are some distinctions between this definition of a function and the one we're forced to use in computer science.

After all, computer science was developed as an extension of mathematics in many ways. It stands to reason that many concepts from mathematics are carried over into computer science.

What are the distinctions between computer science functions? Computer science functions do not have to accept a single argument. They are also not required to listen to any arguments. That will be discussed in a moment. (There are some multivariable functions in higher-level mathematics, but this book does not assume that you are familiar with them.)

Functions in computer science can take zero, one, or multiple arguments. These arguments can then be manipulated in the target data to produce a dynamic function.

This is a parallel. For example, let $f(x) = 3x + 5 = y$. Let's say that we sent in the argument of 3 for this function. We substitute x for 3 since x is the argument and then obtain our final value y. $3(3) + 5 = 9 + 5 = 14 = y$. Therefore, $y = 14$, and our function *returns* the value of 14.

Just as a function can return a value, so can our own functions. These functions can be the end result of all of the math and operations performed in the function. A function, on the other hand, does not have to return anything.

So, what is the point of functions? Functions allow you to abstract specific sections of code in your program that you frequently reuse. From the perspective of a programmer, this has numerous applications, the most important of which is that it makes your code more modular. It simplifies and makes things so that you can start using them in multiple different ways even if you use the same chunk of code over and over again.

Let's think about this for a minute. Assume we require a function that returns the volume of a given rectangular prism. The

The following is how a function is defined in JavaScript:

function functionName(arguments) { // code

return value; // (if necessary)

}

Let's say that we want to develop a function that can return the volume of a prism. The volume of a prism is just length by width by height as follows:

function volumeOfPrism(length, width, height) { return length * width * height;

}

This will give back the value of the volume. This is one of the coolest parts of JavaScript and scripting in general. Just like any other values in JavaScript, you can save this to a variable and use it later. This gives you a lot of utility and flexibility as a programmer. You can also save it outside of a variable and just print the raw value of the function like the following:

document.write(volumeOfPrism(3,4,5));

This will print the value 60. You can save it like the following also:

volume = volumeOfPrism(3,4,5);

This will store the value of volume as 60, which you can then verify by printing it out:

document.write(volume);

Now, with all of that said, let's cover the last topic. We will not cover it entirely in-depth, but it's important that we do so that you will be aware of what you're dealing with.

Object-Oriented Programming: An Introduction

We're not going to get into the intricate coding of object-oriented programming right now. We'll just be dealing with the fundamental concepts of classes and objects. To comprehend these, we must first discuss classes. Some of what we said earlier, such as object wrappers, will make more sense as a result of this.

What exactly is a class? The utility of classes stems from the fact that you may require more complex structures than what the code provides automatically. This is uncommon in programming languages such as JavaScript. At its core, object-oriented programming is about abstraction: the ability to take smaller concepts and integrate them into larger structures that use these concepts.

A better way to think about it is to picture a dog. All dogs share characteristics, such as two eyes, four legs, and a wagging tail. They are also capable of barking. However, there can be significant variation. Dogs, for example, can have different breeds and other characteristics that distinguish them, such as size or weight.

However, there are unifying concepts and properties that apply to all dogs, regardless of breed, size, or weight, and that they all share. Individual data members of a larger structure can be represented by these. This structure is commonly referred to as a dog. These individual data members are referred to as the dog class's properties. Each class may also have standard functions, such as bark or wagTail, that are shared by all instances of the class.

A single instance of a class is known as an object. Each object has its own name and can be treated as a variable in its own right. So, if you define a class called dog, you can create a variable called myDog or any other standard variable name. Then, go to the properties and make any changes you want. The main benefits of object-oriented programming are standardization and abstraction.

As a result, whenever something is referred to as an object, it means that a class was created that is made up of smaller data types and pieces of data that all contribute to the larger concept that is represented both by the object and by its constituent class.

With that, we've covered the majority of what you'll need to know as a new JavaScript programmer.

As a result, learning JavaScript and expanding your knowledge is one of the best things you can do for yourself.

Chapter 4

The Future of JavaScript

You may be wondering, at this point, what the future of JavaScript is. What can I expect to gain from all of this?

JavaScript has been steadily gaining traction since the whitepaper that launched Ajax. Every year, a large number of new JavaScript frameworks are introduced that are fantastic for their various purposes, and more frameworks are expected.

The future of JavaScript is more concerned with your future. JavaScript will only grow in popularity as more features are added to future ECMA standardizations, the web in general becomes more popular, and web platforms mature. Similarly, JavaScript evolves alongside PHP and CSS. JavaScript is expected to continue to evolve in the future.

If you want to be a web developer, you must learn JavaScript and be familiar with its frameworks, as these will allow you to stay current.

JavaScript programmers will become increasingly in demand as technology advances. Several things are currently relegated to other popular scripting languages, such as Python, that can be ported to JavaScript. Natural language processing and machine translation are just two examples of applications that will inevitably be ported to JavaScript, increasing demand.

JavaScript isn't just for making pretty web pages; web page utility is growing. With this in mind, JavaScript will progress to this because web pages can now perform very complex actions. The emergence of browser-based HTML/CSS/JavaScript games only adds to this.

Expect more programmers to be needed in the industry as a JavaScript programmers. As a result, learning JavaScript and expanding your knowledge is one of the best things you can do for yourself.

Conclusion

Thank you for persevering until the end of JavaScript. Let us hope it was informative and provided you with all of the tools you need to achieve your objectives, whatever they may be.

The next step is to put this knowledge to use. Get out there and start experimenting with JavaScript frameworks. Doing it is the best way to reinforce everything you've learned. You won't be familiar with all of them, and you may even be perplexed at times, but if you persevere, I guarantee that it will be worthwhile, and you will emerge as a fantastic web developer.

Finally, if you found this book useful in any way, please leave a review on Amazon!